Towards the Unknown
The Journey into New-Dimensional Consciousness

Dada Gavand

PILGRIMS PUBLISHING
◆ VARANASI ◆

Towards the Unknown
Dada Gavand

Published by
PILGRIMS PUBLISHING

An Imprint of
PILGRIMS BOOK HOUSE
B 27/98 A-8, Nawabganj Road,
Durga Kund, Varanasi 221005, India
Phone: 91-542-2314060
Fax: 91-542-2312456
e-mail: pilgrims@satyam.net.in
Website: www.pilgrimsbooks.com

Copyright © Dada Gavand 2008

ISBN 81-7769-428-6

All Rights Reserved. The contents of this book may not be reproduced, stored or copied in any form — printed, electronic, photocopied or otherwise — except for excerpts used in reviews, without the written permission of the publisher.

Calligraphy
Sahnta Pannutti

This edition typeset by
Astricks
New Delhi, www.astricks.com
Printed in India at
Pilgrims Press Private Limited, Lalpur, Varanasi 221005

First and second editions published by Dada Center Publications
First edition   May 1981   6,000 copies, USA
Second edition   September 2000   2,000 copies, USA
Third edition   January 2008   1,000 copies, Varanasi, India

Acknowledgments

Markell Brooks, you have never missed any opportunity to assist me in my work. For this second book also your encouragement and actual participation in the book project were so very valuable. You were surely a great help in this book production.

Brenda Sales, you and your typewriter were indeed inseparable for quite some time, ever ready to work with me. Your zeal to work on the manuscript, with meticulous care and order, was amazing. You were indeed my right hand on this project.

Nancy Lloyde, with all your preoccupations, you gave much of your time and talent to help me at various stages of the manuscript. Your thoroughness in editing with me was especially valuable. Also your able assistance in typesetting and paste-up was a great help.

Larry Swann, while I was working on this manuscript on your farm in Healdsburg, you took a keen interest in the book project. Your hospitality on the farm to all those who came to assist me was praiseworthy.

Juanita Gilbert, your able assistance in collecting the text from the transcribed talks, and putting the material in order needs special mention. Your art of editing the material made my work easier.

Debby Enrich, you have given a good deal of your time to go over the manuscript with me. Your various suggestions during the editing were useful. I appreciate your help.

Raj Mehta, your interest and encouragement throughout the stages of this project have been helpful.

Maniben Rabadi, your keen interest in this book project and your assistance at various stages of making up the book were a great help.

Shyam Joshi, I am pleased with your work on the drawings which you did for the book, by taking a personal interest.

Sahnta Pannutti, I appreciate your quick response to my call to do the line drawings around the descriptions, as well as your help at paste-up. Your expert hand at calligraphy has added an aesthetic touch to the book.

Paul Koli and Mr. Javed, your contributions towards some of the drawings in the book are appreciated.

Roy Stockman, your interest in the publication of this book in general and in the typesetting in particular was very helpful.

Ken Reed of Wisdom Garden Books, Ruthe Schwarz, Helen and Carroll Wright, and Ginny Cayton, you all have assisted and encouraged me throughout the book project.

Once again Rama Nand was enthusiastic about publishing the third edition of this book. He has worked hard to bring out this edition in a very short time.

Dada

Contents

Acknowledgments — iii
Foreword — vii
The Challenge — x

1. The Emergence of Mind — 1
   Mind, the gift of nature.
   Has the mind arrived at its dead end?
   What is the role of the mind in the nuclear age?

2. Conversion of Consciousness — 12
   How can mind energy be transformed?
   The art of aloof and attentive watchfulness.
   What is the state of the human mind today?

3. Spontaneous Action — 29
   Can there be an action without choice?
   Do you know the intrinsic purpose of life?

4. The Search for God — 42
   Can the mind ever realize God?
   What is the nature of meditation?
   Is it possible to experience divinity?

5. Learning and Intelligence — 61
   Can informative knowledge lead to wisdom?
   How can one learn about life?
   Freedom and bondage.

6. Yoga 77
   Can the fragmented mind ever become whole?
   What is perfect health?
   The death of the mind.

7. The Beauty of Silence 92
   What is the necessity of silence?
   What is creative silence?
   Can the mind be quiet?

8. The Experience of Eternal 108
   Can we experience the totality of life?
   How do we discover the eternal present?
   Are you not divine by nature?

Foreword

There are some people who stand apart. Amidst the crises of society and personal lives, they remain calm and strong. Their words are like shafts of light in darkness: piercing and disturbing, yet illuminating.

Dada is such a man. He touches people's lives. He challenges the basic structure of our existence. His clarity of perception opens the way for the possibility of our own inward vision. Dada's quiet yet intense energy, his sincerity and unique presence are bringing him world-wide friendship and interest in his work.

Early in his life, Dada heeded a demanding internal urge for spiritual understanding. As a young man who had inherited a family business, he became disillusioned with the exclusive nature and binding effect of wealth, prestige, and comfort. Recognizing the dehumanizing effect of commercial culture and surrounding influences, and also the limitation of tradition, he went off by himself in search of the true significance of living. After wandering, and many times of trial and testing, he finally realized to his amazement that the search was indeed totally within.

By being with himself in watchful attention, he faced himself totally. Without following any prescribed discipline, he saw the activity of his own mind very aloofly, and questioned the projections and workings of the entire mechanism of mind.

As Dada says: "I had to be with myself wholly in order to face myself. I was confronted with the play of ceaseless and countless thought-desires. By watching the drama of thought-mind, without getting involved in it or carried away by it, I began to understand the whole content of myself. As I was observing the play of my mind, I suddenly realized that the established pattern of thought-emotion was disturbed, and the whole mind structure was in turmoil. There were no layers, no orderly arranged movements of thought anymore. Intellect and logic lost their validity, and the whole consciousness was in flux. Everything was in intense motion, like boiling water. The ego itself became highly disturbed, agitated and sensitive. I came face-to-face with fear. I had to sense that fear fully and stay with it, without reacting to it. With this challenge, my watchfulness and alertness grew and became much deeper, keeping me in the moment of the present; creating room — a space in my inner being — to absorb the thrust of thought. This was a prelude to change — a jump".

Such — a jump, beyond the mind, appears to be a totally unpredictable and unexpected occurrence. With this change in Dada's life came a tranquility, joy and understanding never known to him before.

Since then, his living has been a sharing of understanding with those seriously interested. This took him to the United States in 1975, where he gave talks and lectures to many different people and groups, in homes and in universities. Dada devoted much of his time to interviews with individuals. He prefers to speak with small groups and individuals, and to communicate on a personal level. He found many eager to explore and find peace in their lives. As they began to see the illusory nature of thought and that their pursuits were based merely on hope, many started looking for new understanding.

Some of these interviews were compiled for his first book, *Beyond the Mind*, published in San Francisco in 1977. In these discussions with people from various walks of life, Dada deals with their serious questions about liberation, family life, emotional problems, sexual energy, creativity, and spiritual growth. He talks openly and directly and points out the basic problem underlying the human predicament.

You, who open this second book, may already be a seeker, a person looking for guidance, truth, peace. There are many books and persons offering various techniques for spiritual growth. But how is the mind, which is in disorder, doubt and conflict, to choose between partial solutions and truth? Dada offers no routines or patterns as exercises. He suggests in this book that you understand the mind mechanism first, before you can use it to search for anything. You use the torch of inquiry to locate and understand the very birth of thought, its intricate moves and all its blind spots.

In reading this book you will feel the presence of a man who sees, somehow, something greater, something more clear than our usual vision. His words are different, they represent something unusual, not the easy answers. His clarity of perception and ability to transmit his vision to the listener are so very unique that it makes him stand apart.

Each chapter represents a talk given by Dada during his three-year stay in the United States. Some adjustment was necessary in taking words spoken spontaneously before informal groups and giving the words structure in written form. The intent was to make it as clear, simple and precise as possible. Dada becomes an artist with words, selecting a poetic style ideally suited to the simple brush-stroke statements. Yet, far from merely a stylized format, it allows the act of reading to become a flow without resistance. Sense this flow, how the eyes and mind play only a part in absorbing the whole of what is being said. The essence is not that which is governed by intellect. Rather, let the essence be absorbed into an unknown part of yourself. Let loose your reliance on the mind and in analysis. Feel, even if only for a moment, this movement without thought, without struggle. Let words emit flashes of feeling, and each line evoke new understanding. Remain open, hesitant and sensitive as you read along. Wait and wonder, to listen in silence, to let the unknown fill you.

The Challenge . . .

With the march of time, the mind of man has come a long way, to become what it is today. It has reached a stage where it can run down the hill and destroy itself, or gather its breath and climb to a new height, with a radical change in the very center of consciousness.

The mind of man is a challenge in itself.

Mind — the layers of past memories, the crystallized structure of thought — is like an organic fossil. This fossil is simply unable to live with the new, incapable of moving with the fresh surging tide of life.

Can this mind be free of its mindness, the material aspect, the hard core of it? Can this mind, the organic fossil, be converted into pure energy — the spirit of life? To flow with the present without any resistance, without conflict?

Putrefaction and fermentation are two opposite biological processes in nature. One leads to decay, destruction and death. The other to conversion, regeneration, and the enrichment of life.

The mind of man has to face this challenge of nature.

Truth, when not understood completely or assimilated and lived honestly, becomes merely information to degenerate into poison: the intellectual arrogance.

Today the mind of man, armed with knowledge, seems to be highly intoxicated with its ego actions. The malady is clear. To work upon one's own mind, to dissolve it and to go beyond, is the only remedial measure before him.

Man's own mind is the ultimate challenge.

Simplicity and humility are the two poles of integrated living. We need integration and not mere education. Real integrity is sanity, order, balance. The integrated mind is simple, honest and sensitive to catch the whisper of intelligence beyond itself.

Such a sensitive energy unit is a new vehicle for a new man, to create a new world. This supreme intelligence alone is the hope and promise for humanity. This new spark of creative wisdom will never be emotionally stimulated, psychologically cultivated or biologically inherited.

It is a discovery for each one, a dimensional jump . . .

The Emergence of Mind

*Thought
Is an exclusive ripple
On creation,
As a wave
Is on profound ocean.*

*A cloud can never fathom the sky,
And a thought can never meet
The highest of the high.*

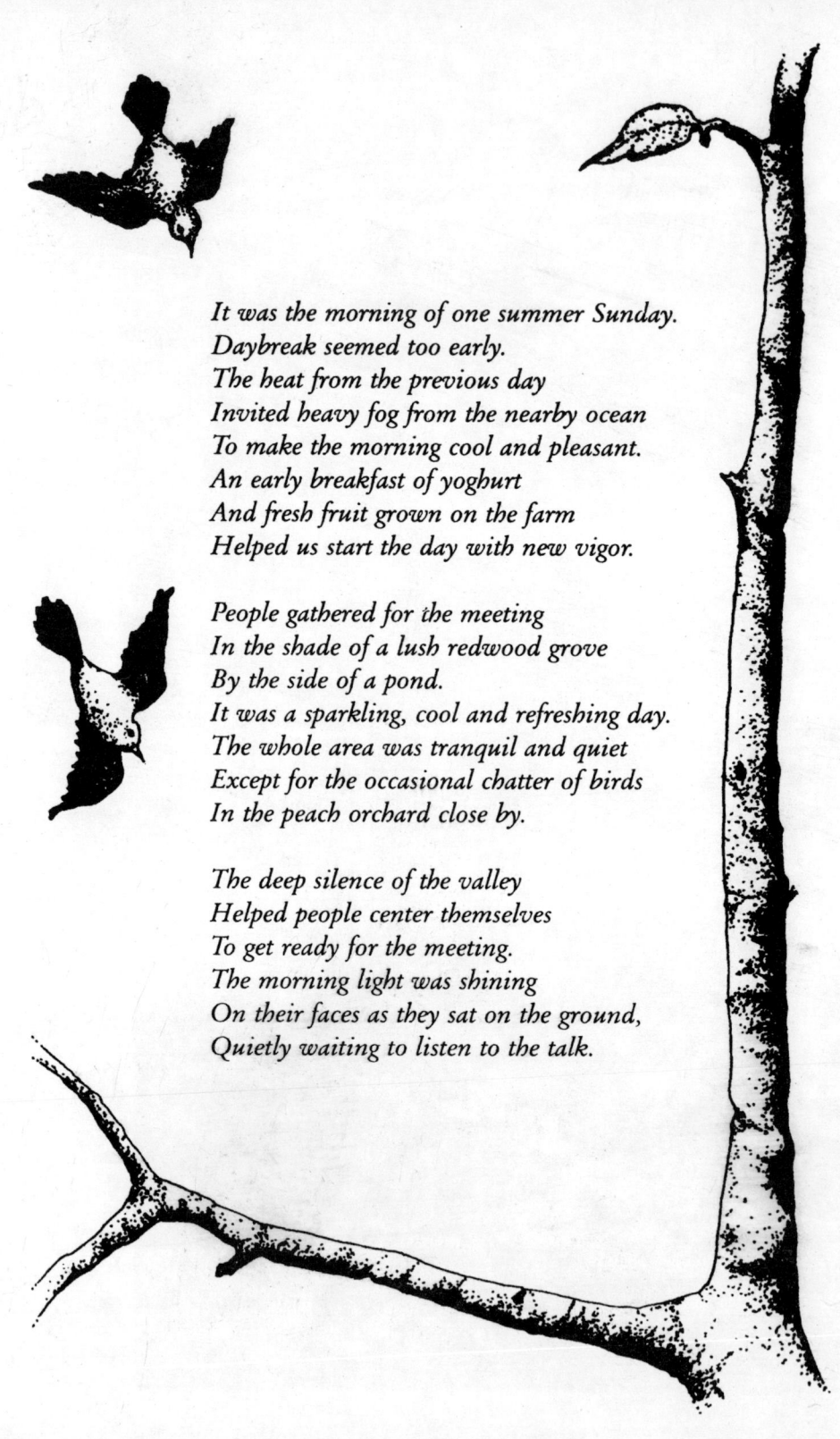

It was the morning of one summer Sunday.
Daybreak seemed too early.
The heat from the previous day
Invited heavy fog from the nearby ocean
To make the morning cool and pleasant.
An early breakfast of yoghurt
And fresh fruit grown on the farm
Helped us start the day with new vigor.

People gathered for the meeting
In the shade of a lush redwood grove
By the side of a pond.
It was a sparkling, cool and refreshing day.
The whole area was tranquil and quiet
Except for the occasional chatter of birds
In the peach orchard close by.

The deep silence of the valley
Helped people center themselves
To get ready for the meeting.
The morning light was shining
On their faces as they sat on the ground,
Quietly waiting to listen to the talk.

1
The Emergence of Mind

Mind, the gift of nature.
Has the mind arrived at its dead end?
What is the role of the mind in the nuclear age?

Is it not true that man is the only creature on earth
Who is gifted with self-consciousness?
He has developed a wonderful apparatus called mind,
The mind with which he thinks, remembers and imagines.
He has really a very beautiful sense of imagination
And the faculty of sharp memory.
With the help of this mind, man has discovered so much
For his own pleasure, his own well-being and education.
This versatile mind of man is a precious gift of nature.

Without the cooperation of nature,
The development of the mind would have been impossible.
Only with the help of this mind
Was man able to survive on the surface of earth.
In the beginning of the human race

Nature was wild, furious and very aggressive.
Every creature had to fight for survival.
The challenge was of self-preservation.

Human beings, as a species, were able to survive
Much more successfully than other creatures
Because of the mind, with its fine imaginative faculty.
They were able to deal with difficult situations,
The problems of survival, the fierce challenges
Of storm, rain, fire, wild beasts, and many more.
With each challenge the mind of man sharpened,
Becoming more clever, versatile, and strong.
In mind, man found a reliable tool for his own education.
Memory was a great blessing to him,
For remembering his experiences and enriching himself.
Memory was surely a tool not only for survival
But also for man's progress.
Many living forms were not able to survive
Because they were not able to think and remember;
They were not able to learn to be so adaptable as man.
Thus many species became extinct.

Because of his capacity to think, remember and discriminate,
Man was able to survive as a species.
He succeeded because the mind, with memory and intellect,
Came into existence to assist in the times of crisis.
Not only did man survive, but he also created a world for himself
Through rational thinking.

Now man has nearly mastered
All the forces and elements of nature.
In gaining this mastery he developed a mind
Which is clever, calculative, imaginative and inventive.

But this mind is now trying to overrule nature,
To dictate and dominate it.
Through this constant struggle for survival,
We have reached a point where the mind has become powerful.
But the human species no longer needs to harbor such fears.
There is no longer the challenge of basic survival.
Yet this fear of destruction and death
Is a constant companion of man even today.
And these fears have led man
To assume the habit of self-centeredness.
Such self-centeredness is a contraction of life energy,
Which is an outcome of the protective devices he employed
To guard himself from dangers all around.

In the deeper layers of memory
And almost in the marrow of his bones,
Man is instinctively self-protective.
The cumulative effect of his experience with wild nature,
Ferocious beasts and other aggressive human beings
Is still dominant in the deeper regions of his consciousness.
Now that our survival as a species is no longer in doubt,
What is the function and purpose of such a mind today?

We see that the mind is still carrying
The heredity of the whole human race.
The inertia of past experiences continues endlessly.
The habitual mechanism of the mind is so strong,
That it is very difficult to change its structure
And to free it from instincts
Developed throughout the march of time.
That is the crystallized structure of the human mind:
An organic fossil in nature.

So there is a struggle now within the mind
Between the inertia of the past and the desire for change,
The desire to have more peace, creativity and relaxation.
Friction develops between the structure of the old
And a vision of the new.
The problem is how to discover that quality
Which we call peace, love and creativity.
As man is more safe and secure now,
He is naturally more interested in discovering
His aesthetic potential.

Can the mind create or experience these aesthetic qualities?
The very struggle of the mind to find these,
Produces divisions, conflicts and new problems.
This struggle itself hinders the experiencing of peace.
It is a peculiar dilemma!

Can the mind, which is a continuity of the old,
Ever discover that which is new, original, ever-changing?
The mind is a result of the past;
Peace and love are expressions of energy in the present.
Only when the energy is fully in the present
Can one experience love and creativity.
The past, the mind, cannot meet the present.
Is it possible to free the mind from its own inertia?
Can the mind free itself from its own structure?
Freedom is the elimination,
The negation of the mind as an entity.
Is the mind ready for its own extinction?
Is the mind interested in its own death?

You want to have love, freedom,
And the experience of the eternal.

For that, you have to pay the price.
Are you ready to pay the right price?
It is not possible to get what you want
By merely desiring it.
If you want a rabbit,
You have to pay the price of a rabbit,
But if you want an elephant,
You have to pay the price of the elephant.
You cannot get the elephant
For the price of the rabbit.
You have got to pay the right price
If you are interested in achieving
The highest aesthetic goals in life.
Are you prepared to pay that much?
Are you willing to accept
The elimination of your thought process?
Are you ready to accept
The death of your own ego, the "I"?
How many of you are really ready?

Look into yourself and find out.
Look very carefully,
For the mind is likely to deceive you
And you will end up in conflict.
So one must be very clear about what the mind is up to.

If you really want to experience love, peace and ecstasy,
You cannot have these with the thought-mind alive.
Either you have one or the other.
You should be very clear on this.
Then you will not make a mistake.
You will not underestimate or overestimate anything.

Towards the Unknown

You will be ready to take the journey
With understanding and clear sight.
Only then will you move into the inner region
Wherein lie all the virtues: love, peace and wisdom.

Ponder and find out if you want to take this journey.
Consult yourself, in quiet alert moments.
This cannot be a dreamy desire
Or an exclusive ambition of the mind.

Finding love and truth is an adventurous journey.
It is like swimming against the current
Of the established social stream,
Of dogmas, traditions and the mind's wishful dreams.
You cannot attain this easily,
Through mere desiring, chanting or praying.

You have to make your own voyage
On this vast ocean of life.
You have to prepare yourself for this unknown journey.
There are no signs on the road;
There is no one to guide you.
You have to start on your own,
Creating your own solitary trail.
Your footprints become your way.

Life is a voyage, a pilgrimage,
On this uncharted ocean of eternity.

You have to be ready all the time,
To face anything that comes along,
Without complaint, without resistance.
You will have to accept any hardship as part of the journey.

There will be no one to complain to.
You will have to accept life as it is.
Acceptance of life as it is, is the beginning.

One has to begin and not think of the end.
You will not know where this voyage will take you.
There is no goal on this journey.
There is no reaching anywhere.
You begin,
And be with that beginning,
That's all.

In beginning lies its own ending,
And in every ending
There is the opportunity for fresh beginning.
This is the whole secret of mindless living,
Heralding the emergence of eternal Being.

Conversion of Consciousness

*It was early spring
And the air was still cool.
The orange groves were laden with fruit,
And the fragrance of orange blossoms
Lingered in the air.
The sun was almost on the western horizon,
And darkness was beginning to settle.
Twilight is the meeting of day and night,
A mingling of moments between darkness and light.*

*As the sun set,
The mountain ridges were aglow
With pink and purple
In stark contrast
With the deepening dark blue of the sky.
The intensity and beauty of nature
Were keenly felt in the quietude of evening.*

*People were walking toward the hall
Through the bountiful orange grove.
It seemed that the quietude of nature
Was reflected upon the faces of the people
As they approached the meeting place.*

The human mind
Is constantly intoxicated
In its ego actions,
Struggling ceaselessly for perfection,
Through its own petty little dreams,
Remaining ignorant
Of life's eternal stream.

2
Conversion of Consciousness

How can mind energy be transformed?
The art of aloof and attentive watchfulness.
What is the state of the human mind today?

Your town of Ojai is a very beautiful place,
Full of green orchards and mountains,
And the ocean not very far.
It seems that nature has poured all its wealth
Into this green little valley.

You have a spiritual mountain like Topatopa
Standing above you,
And many teachers of the time
Visit this place frequently.
It is all so great,
And you are so lucky
To live in this town.
The whole atmosphere,

Conversion of Consciousness   17

The environment, is so beautiful,
And so congenial for the growth of man.

But in spite of all these
Good environmental influences,
Rich associations and aesthetic contacts,
What is the state of man here?
How is he living?
Is he responding rightly to the beauty of nature,
To the existence of ecstasy around?
Or is he only concerned
With his petty little activities
And exclusive pursuits
Of daily routine?

It is interesting to find out.

Are you open, attentive and sensitive
To feel the fullness of living?
Do you know the state of creativity
Wherein one experiences beauty?

Do you have enough love and compassion
To commune with, to experience each other?
To establish communion with yourself
As well as with people around you?

Is not the mind basically self-centered?
Are we not concerned only about ourselves?
Bound by our plans, ambitions, fears and angers?
Do we really need to have this anxiety, worry,

Fear of tomorrow and sense of insecurity
Haunting us all the time?

What is the condition of man today?
What is the quality of the mind of man?
The mind, which is the self, the ego — the "I" —
The whole structure of thought,
Do we know what this all is?

Why are you not free and full of love,
Open and tranquil within?
Do you know what peace in life is,
What order and harmony of energy within are?

In this harmony lies the enrichment of life
Which opens us to ecstasy and contentment
And brings peace and happiness in living.

Tranquility and fullness of living
Are the results of harmonious energy within.
With the discovery of inner balance
We can face any situation in life.
Then we will know what creativity is,
How rich the touch of compassion is.
We will feel the fragrance of real living:
An aesthetic experience of total being.

We don't have that quality, the pristine flow of energy.
Now we are only self-centered and worried,
Caught in habit patterns and routines.
Since early in our childhood
We have learned to behave like this.

Conversion of Consciousness 19

Social and cultural conditioning
Has made us behave the way we do.

Why are we missing balance and harmony
And the totality of unbounded energy?

The mind is constantly striving after something.
And it does not ever accept life as it is.
Thus we miss knowing
What the art of living in contentment is.
We are never at home, never at ease.

Have you ever looked deeply within
To feel and find out all about the mechanism called mind?
How and why it works the way it does?
Or have you always followed it blindly?

Why do you accept this monolithic structure
Of compulsive desires and drives,
This complex, unending chain of thought-mind?
We wrestle throughout life
With worry, fear, anxiety and anger,
And struggle with all the subtle
Compulsions and resistances.

Is it possible to change
This whole structure of mind —
The residue and garbage of the dead past —
To bring about a foundational change?

First we must discover
What this mechanism of mind is,

This ever-active thought-emotion activity.
To change the mind,
We have to know all about it,
By observing it closely and impartially.
Find out why and how this mechanism acts,
And why it works in its habitual patterns
Of likes, dislikes, moods and idiosyncracies.

Why do you cooperate with the mind all the time?
Does it ever bring fulfillment
Of your dreams, your goals?
Or does it only keep you going on and on
In its own perpetual game with shifting pursuits?
Thus you are left running around with hope in time
Throughout your life, until death!

See what this thought activity is:
Each thought is only a fraction of total life movement.
By its very structure and nature,
Thought is a contaminated projection,
Flourishing in antagonism,
Enriching itself in contradiction;
A process of fragmentation,
An exercise in exclusion.

We are full of so many thought images,
Pursuits and goals, fears and hopes.
Loves and angers, compassion and hate,
In different degrees, on various levels,
Opposing each other, and yet
Unmindful of their inherent contradictions.
One thought operates exclusively,
On its own level, in its own corner,

Unaware of the rest of the mind.
We never see the whole circle of mind,
As well as its center,
Functioning as a total unit, at a given time.

We are not aware of the entire cerebral activity:
The whole movement of thought-mind.
One idea, desire or pursuit
Dominates completely at a time,
Making it an exclusive drive of the ego.

Such is the subtle way
And the clever play
Of the age-old mind:
To perpetuate itself in time.

You never know the whole quantum,
The totality of your own energy.
You never act as an integrated being.
You are divided and distorted
By opposing drives and desires.
You are a bundle of illusory goals,
Of exclusive pursuits and disparities
And glaring contradictions.

There is never an action of whole energy,
But only its division by the mind.
No wonder all our lifetime
Energy is spent in hope, fear and friction,
And in solving endless problems.
Can the mind, the thought process,
Ever deal with these problems adequately? Totally?
Thought can help one to escape,

To refuse to see, and to hide.
It can cleverly and wishfully
Postpone an issue.
But on its own level, and with its own efforts,
Thought is incapable of solving problems.

We need to have a different means
To understand, and thus to dissolve,
Psychological and emotional problems
Created by the fragmented mind.

Thought is an exclusive ripple on creation,
As the wave is on the profound ocean.
A cloud can never fathom the sky,
And thought shall never meet
The highest of the high.

The total spontaneous response,
Or the creative action of life energy,
Never can take place through the mind.
The mind is incapable of becoming the whole,
And thus there can be no integrated
And complete action from it.

So we remain fragmented
Throughout our lifetime
And remain incapable
Of reaching our full potential:
The flowering of an integrated human being.
Integrated existence,
Fullness of being,

With spontaneity in acting
Is the true art of living.

The fragmentary nature of thought-mind
Is not going to oblige you
In finding the right action,
Or in experiencing freedom.

Whatever you do, however efficiently you act,
There will always be a division, always a residue
Which again hinders
The oncoming fresh action.

So, how are you going to discover
The totality of your own energy
Which gives fullness to life,
Shows wisdom in living
And leads you to freedom?

First, see the game of the mind:
Its divisive, delusive strategy,
And see how it dissipates life energy.

Be watchful of the game,
Not with the thought,
Not with the intellect,
Nor with a logical conclusion.
But understand the game on its own playground
With attentive perception all around.
To see is to be sensitive.
But now, only the mind sees,
Not the eyes.

It is the mind that hears,
Not the ears.
Now all the senses are dominated
By the thought-mind.

Look at the marvel of life.
There is a new sensing,
Mere attention in the present,
A perception as a witness,
Through which we will discover
A new sensitivity,
Unbiased, intense vitality,
Without the interference of ego — the mind.

Such attention in the moment
Is the beginning of a new direction.
Watchfulness will bring
A new momentum of effortlessness,
A tide of unknown sensitivity,
A unique dynamicity,
Keeping one open, alive and alert
In the freshness of the present.

Eyes and ears will awaken.
Body, brain and nervous system
Will be refreshed and sharpened.
Within the field of watchfulness and alertness,
Your attitude and approach will change.
Life and its expression will be different.
Your whole perspective will be new.

Now you are not sensitive
But merely clever.

You are not open and fresh, but mechanical.
When the compulsion of thought
Makes you act,
There is no total understanding,
But only the rigidity of thought
Which prevents the spontaneous action.
That is the denial of wisdom.

*Choosing between two thoughts
Is not freedom,
Because thought itself is the bondage.*

Now, pure intelligence is not functioning,
But only the one-sided drive of thought.
There is no observation within,
No quietude, no aloofness
Behind your compulsive action.

You have to be awake —
Knowing, sensing, alertly observing
All the moves of thought-mind.

You will see the game simply and aloofly,
Without any motive, without being part of it.
*There will be only an observation,
Without anyone observing.*

Seeing, sensing and aloofly observing
Will guide you through,
Without your getting caught
In the habitual pattern of the mind.

Thus you will gather a new energy
Behind this sensing.
You will be watchfully attentive
To everything outside yourself
As well as within.
This is meditation.

Meditation is not a thought activity.
It is not concentration,
Nor a hopeful mind pursuit.
Meditation is seeing the whole game of the mind
While being aloof and quiet within.

In quietude you will discover
A new sensitivity — uncommitted energy —
Which will guide you to see,
And help you understand
All the activities and subtleties of the mind.

This sensitivity needs energy
For its own consolidation.
It will stay aloof and attentive,
Uninvolved in thought-emotion.

Through this new sensitivity
You will come upon a meditative aloofness,
Wherein you will gather and convert
The life energy now being dominated and used by the mind.
In alert and watchful attention,
Thought activity gets converted
Into sensitivity: a pure life energy
Which pulsates in the now.

Nowness is timelessness,
The beginning and end of time.

You need not go anywhere,
To anyone, to any book
To find this secret of life,
The hidden abode of the unknown.

Right now, in this moment,
By going into yourself,
With attentive watchfulness and with understanding
You can convert thought-energy
And all the subtle movements of the mind.

Conversion of this mind activity
Is the master key
That opens the door
To the inner kingdom.
The whole secret of religion
Is this transmutation of energy:
The dimensional change in consciousness.

This key won't be found in any book,
In any tradition, ancient or most modern.
No one can give it to you
On a silver platter.
Only by your own search,
Unto your own self,
With meditative aloofness,
Can you discover
This magic key.

Towards the Unknown

This inner kingdom
Of new-dimensional existence
Is the gift of the unknown,
And the legacy of human beings,
The birthright of you and me.

Spontaneous Action

*Meditation is not a pursuit
Of any glorified thought,
Or a flight of wishful will,
Nor an enforced silence.*

*Meditation is
Uninvolved all around attention,
Undiluted
By thoughts and emotions,
Unlimited
By techniques and traditions.*

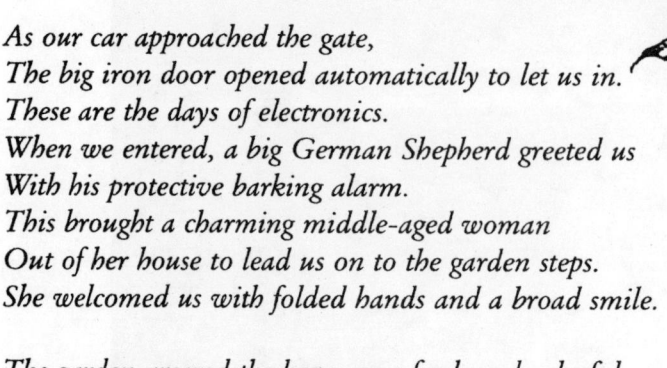

As our car approached the gate,
The big iron door opened automatically to let us in.
These are the days of electronics.
When we entered, a big German Shepherd greeted us
With his protective barking alarm.
This brought a charming middle-aged woman
Out of her house to lead us on to the garden steps.
She welcomed us with folded hands and a broad smile.

The garden around the house was fresh and colorful.
A rectangular patch of dark green turf in the center
Helped to give balance and composition
To the well-laid-out garden.
The inside of the house was as pleasing,
Colorful and aesthetic as the outside.
Every article in the hall was carefully selected
And neatly arranged with great taste.
The lady surely appeared to be a perfectionist.
Binky, the potter and pianist, had built
An artistic abode for herself
With the help of shapes, sounds and colors.

People gathered in the sitting room for the talk.
They were mostly young and eager to understand.
One felt the youthful vitality of the group
As they sat on the floor to listen.

3
Spontaneous Action

Can there be an action without choice?
Do you know the intrinsic purpose of life?

Isn't it important to find out what life is?
To know the basic structure
And nature of this constant energy flow?
Usually we take life for granted
And so never realize the whole beauty of living,
The intuitive aspect and spontaneity of it.

Perhaps we will never come upon that mystery
As we are indulging only in mundane activities.
Routine is not the full expression of living.
That is just one facet of life:
Only the utilitarian part of the living process,
A habitual response of the survival instinct.
Life is much more deep, unknown and profound.
We never venture to fathom this mysterious chasm.
We remain throughout life
Engaged merely with the superficial,
As we are choosing and acting only through thought-mind.

We remain unaware and ignorant,
And fail to experience the wholeness of life,
The creative ecstasy and deeper significance of it.
We are never free from thought-emotion activity
To find the freedom of energy.
Unaware of our conditioning, throughout our lifetime
We remain encaged, trapped on the mundane mechanical level.

Is it possible to discover a meaningful way,
A new understanding for creative living,
Other than the traditional activity of the mind?
Can one unfold the mystery of life?
The creative intelligence of inner being?

To experience the new-dimensional energy,
To discover the mysterious unknown
Is the ultimate challenge.

But the mind keeps us hoping, and projects the promise
Of providing much-needed peace and happiness in life.
Haven't we played enough with hopes, pursuits and goals?
We are frustrated everywhere, never reaching anywhere.

We choose a lifestyle, a mate, a profession.
We choose and act on hope, which is never fulfilled.
Then frustration pushes us to select something "better".
And the entire life span is spent
In hopeful but hopeless pursuits.
Why do we remain unfulfilled throughout life?
We are missing something vital, something precious:
The state of being and the ecstasy of living.

Is it possible to get out of this turmoil
Which is keeping us bound by its own perpetuating game?
Do we realize the bondage of the becoming?
The unending struggle and imaginary goals?
Can you take the initiative —
Not just wishfully and hopefully —
But actually to act upon this bondage
And break its power over you?

To understand its entire structure,
Take a closer look and observe quietly.
Watch closely to understand mind's dreams and demands.
With sensitive, alert openness
Feel the thinker and his thoughts.

Nature has helped us develop a wonderful mind,
With thinking and discriminating ability.
Let us use this capacity to begin
To observe and understand this mind itself.

Begin with the mind.
Look into its workings.
You will soon discover how difficult it is
Even to look at yourself.
You are all the time looking out; you are extroverts.
The mind never likes to see what is going on within itself,
So you are kept totally ignorant about its inner movements.

You know little about yourself —
The hidden motives and blind spots,
Where thought actually takes its shape,
Where desire is very subtly formed.
You are not aware of the origin of thought.

You recognize thought only when it comes out with its thrust
In readiness for action.
You know how to choose between thoughts.
But you never know the real nature
And basic structure of thought.

Thought and action are well-synchronized,
Simultaneous and instantaneous.
There is no gap between thought and action,
No time is allowed to notice the incoming thought.
Thought pushes you out right away into compulsive action.
So you are kept, busy acting all the time,
Thinking that is all your life is — nothing more!

The mind looks out everywhere to investigate.
It likes to find the how and why of everything.
It likes to climb to conquer the highest mountain,
To find the sources of the longest rivers.
The mind wants to investigate the poles of the earth,
The depths of the ocean, the whole structure of the galaxy.

The mind attempts to jump
From ocean depths to galactic heights,
But it never tries to fathom its own hidden source.
Mind, the intellect, attempts to know all and see all,
But abhors looking in, to see its own face.

The mind of man is dense and deep,
With layers of ancient debris.
You never question, you never explore what the mind is.
Do you ever look to see how thought is generated,
Why and from where it springs?

Is thought a valid instrument?
Is it an intelligent expression?

You choose between two thoughts.
Who is making the choice?
Yet another thought, the third one?
Is the third thought trying to choose between the first two?
Do you ever stop to think that all three might be stupid?

Yet you select and act.
You never seem to question this sort of thinking,
Though the source and logic of thought are questionable.

Is it possible to come back,
To watch in one's inner region
How thoughts and desires are constantly manufactured?
Do we ever do that?

We only know acceptance and rejection of thoughts.
We only play with changing patterns of thought.
That is why we are caught up in ideologies,
Philosophies, books — trying to bring about changes
In the outer world, through new thoughts.
We have tried this method for centuries,
And yet where is the basic change in man?
With all the scientific advances,
Philosophical theories and various ideologies,
Are we anywhere nearer to love, happiness and peace?

We still continue to create wars in the name of peace.
This is how the human mind has been living
On the surface of the earth for centuries.

How then are you going to understand life,
Its hidden beauty and true significance?

You have to come back within
To listen and to look at the whole panorama of living;
This ceaseless thought activity,
The inertia of centuries.

You are captured outside, through choice.
Throughout life you keep on choosing.
And where are you with all these choices?
Are you all happy with yourselves?
Have you accomplished your goals through these choices?
You are the end result of all your thoughtful choices.
So are you happy with the buildup of your own image?

You seem to discriminate and to select.
Now I question this very process of selection by the mind.
What is the criterion for your choice?
Maybe just a hope, a wish, a desire, a habit pattern,
Or a compulsion created by environmental influences?

You have to find a way out of the dilemma
Because so far all efforts have failed.
Choosing through thought has not fulfilled life.
Your choice, your selection and education
Have not helped you chisel out
The image of your expectation,
Nor has it all brought
Love, peace and happiness for you.
So what are you going to do if that is true?

You will have to look within
To find out and understand

That mechanism which chooses and discriminates.
How do you choose, and why do you choose?
Who and what is the thing that chooses?
And what is the basis for choice?

Can you take a close look at this mechanism of choice,
Which is based on wishful thinking,
On habits, tradition and fear?

When you clearly perceive the limitations
Of desires, choices, and habits
And thus come back within,
You suddenly discover in your inner sanctuary
A new pulse of sensitivity:
Uncommitted aloof energy.

What will happen if there is no choice,
If this energy is allowed to function freely?
Perhaps this energy, when free and on its own,
Will discover a new spontaneity,
An expression of choiceless action,
Of natural internal intelligence.
In that spontaneity you have no thought, no choice.
It is a positive movement of inner sensitivity,
Which is feelingly attentive to everything around.

When you are intensely sensitive and watchful
To everything within and without,
You begin to see, sense and hear
More sharply and closely, without thought.

This means you become alert.
You are awake, sensitive and alive.

You see and feel without any choice,
Without any will of thought.
Such a state of alert watchfulness,
That state of choiceless perception,
Which is mere attention and anonymous existence,
Is meditation.

Meditation is not concentration of thought.
It is neither prayerful pursuit
Nor a subtle play of will.
Meditation is an intense state of pure attention,
Within and without, with no plans and desires,
No choices or expectations of any sort.

The state of meditation
Is the optimum inner sensitivity,
The absence of thought activity,
Crude and subtle,
Personal as well as impersonal.

When you come upon that internal sensitivity,
That all-around attention of impersonal energy,
The state of meditation comes uninvited.
Then you will never be caught
In any technique of meditation
That is based on practice, or desire and hope in time.

In the state of meditation there is no one to pray to,
Nor is there anyone who prays.
When the mind — the meditator — is not,
The meditation happens naturally.

In that state you are in the present,
Vibrantly alive and alert,

Open and intensely receptive.
Such a state of intense attention,
That anonymity and egolessness,
Is the highest form of prayer.
That is true meditation.

In meditation there is freedom from time.
Such timelessness is an invitation to the supreme,
To the immaculate that resides beyond the mind.

There one remains in the present,
Merged with the flow of the timeless,
Riding the crest of the unknown,
Where all the seekings
And choices of the mind come to an end.

The Search for God

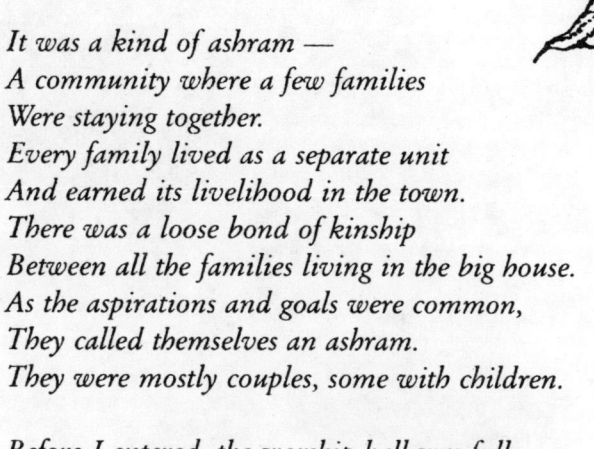

It was a kind of ashram —
A community where a few families
Were staying together.
Every family lived as a separate unit
And earned its livelihood in the town.
There was a loose bond of kinship
Between all the families living in the big house.
As the aspirations and goals were common,
They called themselves an ashram.
They were mostly couples, some with children.

Before I entered, the worship hall was full,
Everyone sitting in a line in lotus pose.
There was a deep silence and a feeling of serenity.
The chanting had just finished,
And all were eager to hear the discourse.
There was an eagerness on their faces to learn more
Than what they already knew
About the deities of their worship.

To reach God was their objective.
They had a strong feeling, almost a passion
To achieve this goal.
A mild Eastern incense permeated the hall,
Enhancing the feeling of purity and religiousness.

Right here,
Beyond the frontiers of mind,
Across the region of time,
Into the sanctuary of silence,
Resides the supreme intelligence,
My Lord
The timeless divine.

4

The Search for God

Can the mind ever realize God?
What is the nature of meditation?
Is it possible to experience divinity?

Friends,
I see your great interest in living as a community
And in chanting and prayers as a group activity.
I see your eagerness to find the Lord,
To know what Shiva is, what God is.
I am glad to see your devotion,
And your sincerity to attain the goal.

I think everyone has to discover for himself
That quality of Godhood, that immaculate timeless state,
The internal touch of divinity,
So that our lives will be happy, creative and free,
Full with love, peace and divine grace.

One must have the right means
To fulfill the right end.

The Search for God

It is important how you proceed
To discover this divine grace.
The first step is as important
As the last one, is it not?

So how are you going to begin
Your search for God?
See what happens
When you become interested in finding God.
Immediately a part of the mind responds
With an image, a picture,
A feeling and a desire.

You have read and been told
Many stories and descriptions of God —
How he looks, where he lives,
What he likes and dislikes
And what he expects of human beings.

Don't we have images about God?
Fanciful as well as rational?
Carved by hands and minds?

The mind has the tendency to create an image
Of anything that is unknown to it,
And also has the capacity to pursue that image.

But is God only an idea,
An image created by the mind?
Can the mind ever know
What God is? What timelessness is?
Can thought ever experience God?
It is interesting to find out

How the mind is attempting
To know, to experience God
Through its speculative desires.

The mind is eager to know
So many things of the world.
And also the idea which the mind calls God
Becomes one more object
Of its interest and pursuit.

You refer to books
And follow traditions,
And come out with descriptions,
Vivid imaginations of a God
Based on ancient speculative ideas
And your personal fears and hopes.
So there begins a new excitement
And renewed search by the mind to find God.

Do you know what this mind is?
The very instrument
With which you are trying to know God?
Let us ponder a while to find out.

Wait and watch,
Closely and quietly,
To discover a marvel of nature —
The structure and pattern of thought-mind.

Thought-mind conceptualizes everything.
It speculates all the time,
Uses ideas, creates images,

And then tries to follow them,
Thus creating a psychological future.

Thought creates a goal in space
To be fulfilled in the future.
The projection of mind is time.

The mind is nothing
But the instrument of imagination,
The creator of hope
That struggles in time.

If you look into yourself
You will see how many images,
Concepts and theories
You harbor in the head.

The mind is a storehouse
As well as a fountain
Flowing with memories
Of incomplete hopes and unfulfilled dreams.

The imaginative and fragmentary mind
Can never discover
That dynamic, effervescent energy
Of eternal, timeless quality.
The mind is the product of time,
Whereas Godhood is timeless divine.

The dead past cannot contact
The living present.
Time cannot contact the timeless.

Shadow cannot contact light.
Contracted polarity cannot contact enormity.

Mind is the inertia of the dead past,
The memories that are gone and over,
Nonexistent in fact.

See what the mind is first,
Its illusory nature and its limitations,
Before you try to find God
Through the mind.

See what the cultures
And traditions have done,
What the religious reformers
And moralists have attempted.

They have divided the mind
Into good and bad,
Pure and impure,
Without taking the trouble to understand
The basic structure of it,
The exclusive nature of it.

We have only culturally based images
And traditional patterns of morality
Through which we believe
What is goodness, religiousness and sanctity.

The pattern of morality changes
From time to time,
From generation to generation,
And from country to country.

We strive our whole lifetime
To be good and religious,
According to the cultural patterns
And the religious dogma of the day,
So that we can find God.

Now ponder a little.
See how with this illusory process
The mind works to change itself,
By imitating the laid-down patterns.

Is this mind ever going to be good?
Can we bring about goodness
In the whole mind,
In the entire complex structure
Of thought-emotion activity?

Find out.
Watch your own mind.
See just how good it is,
How obedient it is.

Can one arrive at ultimate goodness
By bringing about superficial changes
In conceptual and cultural patterns
In this ancient monolithic mind?

How much do we know
About our own mind?
Are we going to make it good
Without understanding all its contents?

The mind is hidden
And difficult to know.
It is as crystallized
And as ancient
As the Rocky Mountains
And the mighty Himalayas.

It has deceived us for centuries
By trying to make itself good.
But it cannot oblige you
By being good and peaceful enough
To find God.

A thought struggling to silence the mind,
Is as the wave trying to pacify the ocean.
The partial attempting
To purify the total,
How on earth is this possible!

See the fallacy of the mind
In its wishful, illusory pursuit —
The mind trying to become good,
To contact that ultimate goodness
Which is God, divinity, the eternal spirit.
Perhaps any activity of thought
Trying to know the divine spirit
Is the hindrance to experiencing God.

Ignorantly and ironically
The mind works as a hindrance
And perpetuates itself
By indulging in the thought-emotion mechanism
And in its endless plans and pursuits.

You never look at yourselves
Very closely and objectively,
To understand this hindrance of exclusive
And ceaseless cerebral activity.

Observe all the movements of the mind —
Its images, sensations and dreams.
See how they are entrenched in the past.
Look at how they follow a wishful path,
Creating contradictions and divisions in thought.

The mind is interested
Only in its own continuance.
It craves for constant dominance.
The mind finds its sustenance
In excitements and sensations.

So understand this crystallized structure
On all levels first.
Take the total challenge
Of this whole mind mechanism
Before you use it to search for anything.
You hope to use the mind
As an instrument, a vehicle
To lead you toward the experience of God!
See its inadequacy!

At the cost of your own life force
The mind is misusing energy,
Scattering it everywhere
In a very clever and subtle way,
In petty little pursuits
And self-intoxicating drives.

Through thoughts and various drives,
The mind uses this vital force
To fulfill its immediate objectives
And long-term goals.

In freedom from the dominant thought process
Lies the liberation of your vital force,
The purity of life energy
And the emergence of intelligence.

Liberation of energy
Leads to the experience of divinity.
He who is mukta — liberated —
Is in communion with divinity — with God.

Only in this very unique
And mystical state of free energy
Can you experience the supreme,
The eternal timeless being.

It is not possible at all for the thought process
To lead you to the experience of Godhood.
This is not the business of the mind,
So let the mind realize this fact once and for all!

All pursuits of thought
Must come to an end.
Seeing this fact is the first step
Toward inner quietude and peace.

By close and alert watching
Of all the movements of body and mind,
You will discover that
The constant ripples of thought

On our life energy
Are the cause of disquiet.

Is it possible
To bring about the tranquility,
A sense of fullness and serenity,
In total mind energy?

Be passionately vigilant,
Attentive within yourself on all levels.
Watch aloofly and understand
This ever-busy thought movement.

To bring about total quietude,
Be alertly attentive to the disquietude
In all its hidden corners,
On all levels of the self.

The agitated and disturbed energy
Will never know serenity.
In deeper depths of tranquility
Hides the unbounded divinity.

When the mind is quiet
And the senses remain tranquil,
You will feel the beauty
Of the inner divine.

All imagery of the mind
Has to come to an end.
No prayers or supplications are useful,
Neither chanting nor dancing is helpful.

Absolutely no words from any scripture
Nor images are necessary.
To feel His presence, the mind must be absent.

We cannot bring about this total silence
Through repetitive phrases,
By dulling or lulling ourselves
Through concentration or contraction,
Or by escaping through images.

Silence is not a passive state
Bordering on sleep.
Rather, it is a very dynamic and potent existence.
It is intensely watchful,
Sensitive and meditative,
An attentive, effervescent state
In one's own inner space.

A spiritual person is happy, vibrant and alert,
Active, meditative and creative,
Yet serene and quiet within.

When we are completely silent
On all levels of our being,
In all parts of the personality —
Only then is there the possibility
Of experiencing divinity:
The timeless existence —
The touch of the unknown.

Silence is the gate
To enter within,

And the inner domain
Is the kingdom of divinity.

He who is alertly silent,
And attentive in each moment
Is in constant meditation.

Meditation is not concentration,
Not the focusing of the mind,
Willfully, hopefully or fearfully,
On some fixed point or image.

Concentration is merely contraction,
A limitation of the vision
And a narrowing down of the life force.

Meditation is a flow
Of heightened sensitivity,
With intense alertness
And extensive awareness
Within the whole field of mind activity.

In such a mobile meditation
You can catch the pulse of pure energy:
The flow of timelessness.

When one is awake into oneself
And highly sensitive
On all levels of existence,
One discovers a uniquely potent vibrant energy.

Then the whole being becomes sensitive,
Alert and extensive,

Without being dominated
By ideas of the thought-mind.

You begin to move with the moment.
You experience the vibrant present,
A unique state of freedom
Untouched by time and tradition.

So see what the mind does
When it creates an image of God.
The image of God is not God.
It is just a concept.
This flight of the imagination
Creates a synthetic image,
A bubble in the air.

And you can create as many
Colorful bubbles as you want
In the realm of the imaginative mind,
With the excitement of wishful thought.

Imagination is the mind game.
It is the flight of energy
From the center
To the periphery.

Thought always takes energy
Away from the center,
Limiting it, dominating it,
For its play on the circumference.

Living is only an interaction
Of thoughts and emotions.

The world is simply a play of thoughts,
Their wishful pursuits and sensations,
And their reactions on the circumference.

The primary necessity
Is to bring the whole energy
Back into yourself, by freeing it
From all the images of the mind.

Even the image of God
Created by a wishful mind
Is merely an idea in space.
It is a hindrance, a postponement,
To experiencing divinity.

The mind has to be purged
Of all its pictures and pursuits,
All its hopes and fears
And so-called personal but exclusive experiences.

Stop the energy dissipation.
Remain silent, attentive and anonymous.
It is the inner sensitivity and humility
Which will lead you to divinity.

You cannot meet God through the mind,
Nor experience the timeless through time.
Thought cannot meet the omniscient.
The eternal cannot touch the transient.

Only with freedom from thought
And from mental cravings and ambitions

Does the energy become
Whole, tranquil and pure.

Such inner purity and humility
Will invite the hidden divinity.

The pure consolidated energy,
With its silence and fullness within,
Awaits in readiness to meet the divine,
To experience that which is beyond the mind.

There across the region of time,
Beyond the frontiers of the mind,
Within the sanctuary of silence
Resides the supreme intelligence,
Your Lord, the timeless divine.

Learning and Intelligence

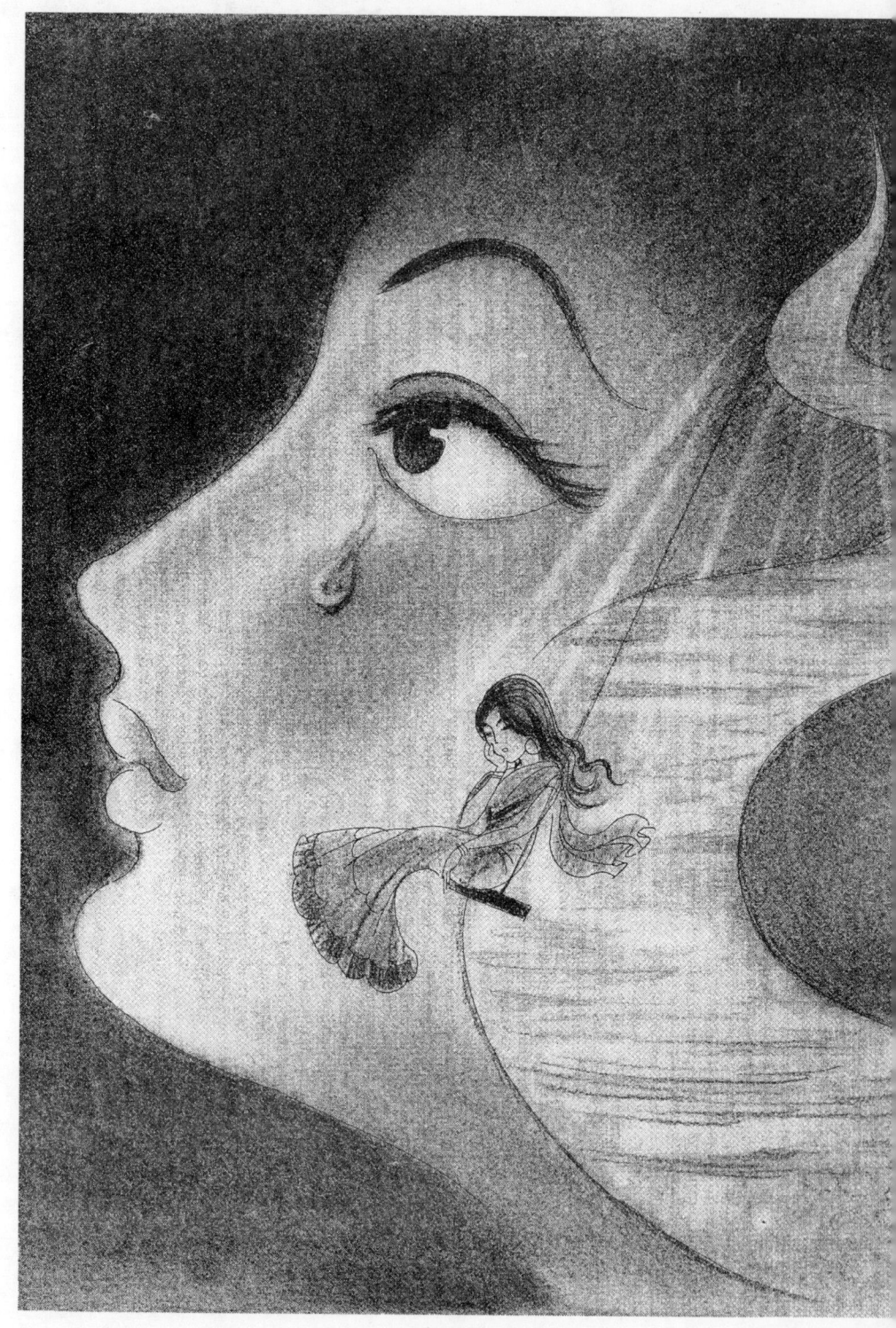

People are sad
Over the past,
Fearful and doubtful
About the future,
And ceaselessly restless
In the present.

No wonder,
In constant anxiety of living
They miss
The perfume of the present —
The unending eternal moment.

A heavy fog was rolling over the San Francisco Bay
As we crossed the Golden Gate Bridge into the city.
Grayness enclosed us, cutting off sight
Of the expanse of ocean beyond the bridge.
The wind-tossed great pines that edge the city
Were barely visible through the thick cold blanket.
A penetrating chill followed the moving mist.

We arrived at the warm home of a young couple,
A flat in a neatly painted Victorian house,
High atop one of the city's steep hills.
The living room was cozy and comfortable,
Furnished simply with Indian fabrics,
With cushions and an Oriental-style rug.

Most of those gathered for the meeting
Were seekers and yoga teachers.
They considered themselves
To be following a spiritual path;
They were experimenting with many techniques
And listening to different teachers.
In manner they looked calm, gentle and serene.
All of them sat upon the colorful carpet
And seemed anxious to hear the evening talk.

5

Learning and Intelligence

Can informative knowledge lead to wisdom?
How can one learn about life?
Freedom and bondage.

Dada:
What shall we talk about this evening?

Questioner:
Some of us have heard your talks before,
But there are others who haven't heard any talks at all.
So maybe you can give us some of your background.

Dada:
You would like to know my background?
You mean what I stand for, what I represent?

Questioner:
Yes, it's very new to some of us.

Dada:
I am glad you feel it is new.

The new is always unknown.
Therefore you are eager and open to understand,
And more attentive to know about it.

In fact, I don't have any ideological stand.
I don't have any philosophy as such,
Neither a tradition nor a religion.
I don't even read books.
It may sound a little strange, but it's true.
I don't accept and follow any tradition, old or new.
Nor do I have any technique to offer you.

Questioner:
How did you learn what you teach?

Dada:
Learning is a constant movement.
In freedom from thought,
In unbiased, alert attention of total life energy,
One finds the instrument of learning.

One learns and understands
Spontaneously and intuitively
Within one's own energy field.

Questioner:
And how did you come upon it?
How did you learn all that you understand?

Dada:
I looked into the working of my mind,
Pondered, questioned, searched,
Meditated and discovered my blind spots
In thinking and feeling.

I found to my amazement
The compulsive pressures
Of strong traditional influences
And environmental conditionings.
I discovered the play of habit patterns
Very subtly working inside of me.

I found that what I called myself, "me",
Was not a cohesive or integrated entity,
But a loose bundle of various thoughts and memories:
Rational, as well as irrational longings,
Practical, as well as crazy pursuits.
I watched in myself and discovered
That the demands, doubts and deceptions,
Cleverness, cruelty and compassion,
Good as well as bad, were co-existing
And were merrily mingling together.
All the attitudes and objectives of my mind
Were apparently functioning at ease,
Yet intrinsically acting in contradiction and conflict.

I stopped and wondered,
Watched within and understood.
From my chattering mind
I learned how mechanical and traditional
Were my thinking and feelings.
I also perceived how a part of myself,
Deep down into my center,
Is mysteriously very much silent, unperturbed,
And aloof from all the outer happenings.
From my clever and logical mind
I learned how futile the informative knowledge is,
And thus I learned the art
Of being in the state of not-knowingness.

To be innocent is to be open, sensitive and receptive
To the whisper of intuitive intelligence.
To be in the state of not-knowing
Is the highest art of knowing.
The whole secret of life is there.

But the difficulty is that
We know too much, too many facts.
The mind is just flooded with information.

It knows all about itself
And about other people as well.
The mind thinks it knows about life,
Reality and God, too.

The mind assumes that it knows all.
It is a miniature storehouse,
A verbal-and-psychological encyclopedia.

You think you know everything
And use this information
To formulate exclusive opinions
And make convenient conclusions
About yourself and others,
About life and its purpose.

Can your logic,
Based on mere information
Which you have read and heard,
Give you the understanding
And experience of life?

What have you got of your own?
Do you have your own experience,
Or is it all borrowed from others?
Watch and look into the workings of your mind.

Have you any genuine understanding?
Find out if you really know anything
As a direct experience of life.

The mind will not accept the fact
That it has no direct experience of life.
All its theories are based on speculation.
Its opinions and ideologies
Are shelters of convenience and convention.

Perhaps this very knowledge —
Which is but the accumulation of information —
Is a real hindrance
In directly experiencing the fullness of life.

What is real knowing?
What is realization?

How do you know a bird?
Is it not through idea?
You recognize it from memory
And describe it with words.

You find its name from memory,
"This is a beautiful peacock".

You recognize the bird,
But is recognizing or describing
An actual experiencing?

You never see it freshly, openly, and fully.
When you look at it,
You identify it immediately
With the idea, mere words.

The mind does not see and meet
The peacock as it is.
The mind is simply incapable
Of meeting and experiencing the bird
Directly and fully in a fresh moment.

To know the peacock
Is to be in communion with it.
Such knowing is experiencing,
Which is a direct contact with total energy.

To be in communion with anything,
Mind — the idea activity — has to remain quiet.
Only in silence does communion happen.
There, knowing and experiencing become one.

The mind can only interpret and describe,
Thus it will never be able to experience
On a deeper level,
On a fuller dimension of existence.
As long as there is thought movement
There shall not be communion with anything.

What we usually call understanding
Is basically an intellectual conclusive process,
A logical assertion of thought,
Not an experiencing of full energy.

We speculate and conclude immediately,
According to our own bias,
In response to our personal background,
Never establishing communion, or direct contact.

Isn't it the same with one's self?
Do you have direct contact with your self,
With the I, the mind?
Do you know yourself exactly as you are?

Does not the mind simply speculate about itself?
Is it not self-centered, divided against itself?
Is it not highly biased and prejudiced?

Look at your mind's
Constantly changing thought movements,
Its roots deep in the past.
See the nature of thought,
Its origin, content and flights.
See the dead ends and deceptions,
Its blind spots and frustrations.

Thought is a biased reaction
To the influences and challenges of life.
There is never a moment without thought.
Every action is an outcome of compulsive thought.

The agent, the interpreter,
The conceptual activity — which is the mind —
Is the troublemaker,
The creator of ill will and misunderstanding,
The source of all sorrow and suffering.

*Can one be free of thought
And yet be attentive and sensitive
To things, people and situations?*

Can one's life energy
Meet the other energy
Directly and spontaneously
Without the agency of thought?

*But, we are rooted in the past,
And dream about the future,
Thus missing the present.*

We are sad about our past,
Fearful and doubtful about the future,
And ceaselessly restless in the present.
No wonder,
In constant anxiety of living
We miss the perfume of the present,
The unending eternal moment.

The thought process, which is idea activity,
Is the inertia of the past.
Only in imagination
Does the psychological future exist.

Worry over past and future
Consumes the energy of life,
So you expend and run short of energy
To be utilized in the present.

When there is no thought of any sort,
Is there any past or future at all?
The idea divides energy, creating psychological time.
The elimination of mind is freedom from time.

You have taken thought for granted
And entertained it all along.
Have you ever questioned the validity
Of this constant thought activity?

From childhood you were trained
To select, polish and obey thought;
To choose, accumulate and glorify thought.
Your prayers, worships and God images, too,
Are wishful pursuits of your own thought.

Don't you ever feel disgusted
With your own thought process,
An energy-draining activity,
A constant obsession and burden?

Have you ever looked meditatively
Into the cause and effect of thought,
Into the birth and death of thought,
The cycle that creates fear and conflict
With resultant sorrow?

Every expression of thought-emotion
Consumes psychic force,
And every projection of thought
Drains the vital source.

Each one is blessed with a specific unit
Of valuable life energy.
Constant depletion of your energy
Through the mechanical activity
Of chronic and compulsive habit patterns
Is utterly stupid and in vain.

Indiscriminate and ceaseless psychic activity
Results in energy dissipation,
Causes mental exhaustion
And invites psychosomatic disorders.

Very few thoughts are necessary
For daily living and functioning.
One need not use thought
When it is not necessary.
Thought need not function automatically.

But now, there is no ending of thought,
Even when we retire to bed.
Surprisingly, in sleep, too,
The thought process goes on and on.
The mind projects fantasies and fears,
And even while asleep,
It indulges in unfulfilled plans and pursuits.
This wishful play of mind is constant and continuous.
Living is nothing more than this chain of thoughts!

Like the pumping of the heart,
The mind remains ever active
Throughout the lifetime,
Busily creating and then trying to solve conflicts.

We are rarely at ease
And never at fully tranquil rest.
Constant anxiety and dread of the future
Cause mental conflict and distress
And various psychosomatic diseases.

Then we go to psychiatrists,
Visit all kinds of therapists,
But never discover the secret
Of inner tranquility and peace.

Your whole energy can remain
In its fullness, in its tranquility,
To experience peace and profundity.

Tranquil energy of the inner domain,
Unhindered, uncontaminated by mind,
Is a potent intelligent force.
It is a new-dimensional energy source.

You think that you use thought,
But I doubt it.
It is thought that uses you,
Uses your life energy,
By dominating, grabbing and dictating to it,
And by possessing people and things.

Thought is a possessive, aggressive, dominant force,
Subduing and hindering the creative source.

Realizing the limitation of thought,
Its exclusive pursuits and mediocre nature,
Mechanical habit patterns and subtle compulsions,
Is understanding.
It is the beginning
Of the awakening of intuitive intelligence.

The world needs the discovery of such intelligence
To experience a new-dimensional existence:
A path of impersonal understanding,
A way of happy and creative living,
The life of freedom and peace.

Meditative watchfulness generates a new insight,
Keeping one free, independent and whole within,
To function spontaneously as a creative being.
Then within the field of human sensitivity,
A new energy source will emerge.
The dawn of a new impersonal intelligence
Shall swell and burst within the heart.

Suddenly on the horizon of inner space
The mystery and marvel of unknown being will appear.
The hidden glory and touch of divinity
Will be experienced as ONE, without the other.

Such a benediction of sublime intelligence
Is a supreme promise for each of us, here and now.

Yoga

Virtue?
Is not the behavior pattern
Of the mind,
Nor a goal in view,
Or an achievement in time.
Virtue is a flower
That blooms in the present.
Virtue is the fragrance
Of a timeless moment.

Far from the city, out in the valley,
It was springtime.
Mountains were blossoming with wildflowers.
The weather was still cool, but hot springs
In the valley created a blanket of warmth
To make the cold bearable and pleasant.
The place was green, shady and quiet.
Occasional gusts of wind brought a mild smell
Of sulphur from the hot springs nearby.

It was a Yoga Seminar.
Most of the people who came were teachers of yoga,
And others were interested in health,
Nutrition and New Age living.
There was an attitude of discipline in the movements
Of the people who sat on the floor to listen.
The orderliness had a ring of enforcement to it.
A few incense sticks were burning in the room,
And the mild fragrance mellowed the silence.

The meeting room was full, the people quiet.
Everyone was sitting in lotus pose with spines straight,
Yet a few were keen to find places
To lean against the wall.

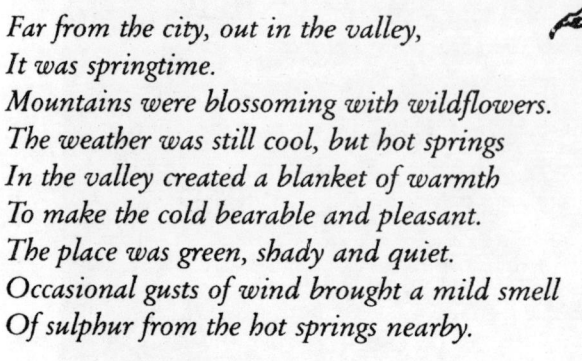

6
Yoga

Can the fragmented mind ever become whole?
What is perfect health?
The death of the mind.

What is yoga?
Yoga means "union".

We interpret that word in many different ways:
A union between mind and body,
Between lower and higher self — union of man with God.
But this is a convenient interpretation by thought-mind.

I doubt if there is any such thing as a union
Between the lower self and the higher one!
Can lower and higher ever unite?
Do darkness and light ever meet?

Can the past ever live with the present?
Can the mundane absorb the immaculate?

Can time move in the timeless?
Or ignorance ever contain intelligence?

Yoga simply means union,
A union of life force,
Union and integration of energy,
A unity within, wholeness, holiness.

We view yoga as a means
To union with God,
A union with this or that.
But this union is not with anything.

All life energy has to be united,
For now our energy is divided,
Fragmented and scattered everywhere,
In thousands of conflicting drives and desires.

Are we aware of our divided energy —
Physical, mental, emotional, spiritual,
And various subdivisions
Through thoughts and ideas?

The mind divides itself in fragments
And then aspires to meet
The highest of its imagination.
How I wish that were possible!

The purpose of yoga
Is to discover
The inherent integrity of life force,
To experience energy as a whole.

Then this whole energy quantum acts
In its own independent and mysterious way.
Energy finds its intuitive expression,
Which is spiritual action.

We are not integrated and whole beings yet.
We are basically divided, fragmented,
Working on different levels,
Living in exclusive compartments.

The fragmented mind is unable to sustain
The whole force of life energy.
The profundity of total energy
 Is too much for thought-mind.

Is thought a parasite?
Does the mind use energy
For its exclusive existence,
 To sustain its own roots?

No wonder the mind divides energy
To use it bit by bit.
Channeling the whole life force
Is a clever trick of this "I".

Elimination of this division
Through understanding
Brings about cohesion,
The wholeness of life energy.

The totality of energy is perfection,
The excellence.

Therein lies true intelligence,
The wisdom of life,

While fragmentation of energy —
Uncoordination,
Unwholeness —
Is ignorance.

Do you see this fact,
How we fragment the energy,
Limit our understanding,
And create problems everywhere?

Can we discover the totality of being,
The wholeness of energy within?
The yogi is one who is unfragmented,
Contented and fully centered within.

See what you have done to yourself:
Past and future — likes and dislikes —
Good and evil — pleasure and pain.
Can you see this divisive game?

Can you look at your mind
To find out how it works
Through isolative divisions
And fragmented perceptions?

Thought dominates energy on one level,
With the exclusive pursuit of an idea.
Fragmentary thought is a trick of the mind
To negate the wholeness of life force.

Idea is an activity of exclusion,
A fragmented drive of energy,
A piecemeal approach to life,
A cause of ignorance and strife.

The mind is constantly occupied.
We harbor so many thoughts,
Desires, ideas, ambitions, etc.
God knows how many there are!

We often change our ambitions,
Our moods and pursuits of sensations.
We are composed of a thousand fragments,
Each pushing us in a different direction.

Yoga is a way of cohesion,
A means to unite the whole energy.
But mostly mind and body are kept busy
Working on physical fitness alone.

You are concerned about health,
Disease, fatigue and tension.
So you use yoga for health and relaxation only,
And never attempt to go beyond them.

Good physical health and a sense of well-being
Are absolutely necessary.
But after health, relaxation and leisure,
What next?

When one is at ease and undivided,
One is in perfectly good health.

Health is energy in its fullness.
Perfect health is the feeling of wholeness.

From that wholeness
Emerges true balance and equanimity,
A new and unique order of energy.
But we do not know that quality.

We remain "seriously" busy,
Concerned with physical body,
Diet, exercise and relaxation,
And never transcend this level.

Mere seriousness about life is not enough.
It can make one exclusive,
Can condense and contract the vision.
Be aware of such exclusion.

It is essential to be intelligent,
Not merely to be serious.
A yogi is one who is open,
Meeting life intelligently, without a barrier.

The mechanistic mind with its habits
Is not interested in anything but in itself.
Continuity of the status quo at any cost
Is its vested interest and objective.

Look into yourself to watch.
Be attentive to every thought.
Be aware of the mind's escapist flights,
Its hidings, seekings and divisive drives.

In wholeness of energy
There is no room for the mind.
In totality of being with its spontaneity
Lies the death of the thought-mind.

See through attentive watchfulness
How cleverly and subtly
The mind obscures and denies
The wholeness of life energy.

In meditative attention
You bring to an end
The perpetual mechanical thrust
Of the cycle of mind.

It is fun to watch
The constant stream of thought
Whirling around with its protective shield
In mind's energy field.

To witness the movement of thought,
Very quietly, as it moves in oneself,
As a fact of that moment,
Is not a concept, but an experience.

In aloof perception, idea is dissolved,
And only observation remains.
Instantaneous understanding takes place
In uninvolved observation of the moment.

In alert and attentive perception
Energy dissipation is arrested.

The energy is gathered within
To stay at home, tranquil and serene.

Consolidated energy in the inner domain
Experiences the unpredictable fleeting mystery
That moves with the moment
And is ever fresh and new.

But you never look into yourself
With aloof and fresh attention.
How you are carried away by thought
Day after day, till the end of life!

You never experience, and so never understand
The structure of thought,
The cleverness and ignorance of thought,
The birth and death of thought.

The more clever you are,
The busier you become,
The more progressive and modern you look —
How excited and elated you feel!

We do not know
The spiritual dimension.
Our living is automatic action
Of constant thought projection.

To be busy constantly
Is a call of education and culture,
A compulsion of competitive society,
Greed crystallized into habit.

Restlessness and busyness
Are the reactions of mind activity.
Tranquility and quietude
Are the actions of pure energy.

Do you know the state of silence,
The tranquil energy of inner space?
How active and effervescent silence is,
How dynamic and creative that state is?

Peace is not absence of action.
Quietude is not mere nothingness.
Silence is not passive existence,
Nor an interval between two acts.

Silence is sensitive and dynamic,
A movement of pure energy within,
Attentively awaiting in inner space
To greet the dawn of divine grace.

In alert and watchful inner space,
In the net of attentive awareness,
Catch the outgoing thought
Before it affects and excites.

Locate the trajectory of thought
As it moves out.
Watch and catch the idea at its birth,
Before it takes its root.

Come back, come close.
Enter deep within yourself.

Watch, observe and locate
How every thought takes its shape.

To watch within the energy field
Aloofly, without any choice,
To observe the play of mind without any intention
Is the right way of meditation.

Meditation is not
A pursuit of glorified thought,
Or a flight of wishful will,
Nor an enforced silence.

Meditation is choiceless perception —
Uninvolved, all-around attention,
Undiluted by thoughts and emotions,
Unlimited by technique and tradition.

Without any goal in mind
Or desire to change in time,
Remain in watchful alertness.
Be a stranger, an aloof witness.

In silence of the senses
And tranquility within,
You discover the mystery
Of total being.

The true yogi is one
Who lives in total freedom,
Beyond time and tradition,
Rooted in his internal kingdom.

The totality of inner being
Is a new-dimensional experience,
A discovery of new existence,
A transformation and fulfillment.

The Beauty of Silence

The secluded, well-to-do community
Was set back off the highway in the wooded hills,
Away from the noisy city, out toward the ocean.
A winding road took us up and up slowly,
To the house sheltered by the shade of green trees.
A cluster of tall, massive redwoods
Overlooking the house stood like sentinels.
The redwoods looked majestically quiet and aloof,
Powerfully alive in their massive growth.
Two of the redwoods looked so old
That they must have been as ancient
As the time of the birth of Buddha and Christ.

The wooded grove around the house was dark and cool,
And even inside the house one could feel the dampness.
A large window in the meeting room
Showed the greenery of forest
Through which only a few rays of sun could enter.

People who sat in the crowded room
Were artists and seekers,
As well as intellectuals and businessmen.
They chatted nervously until the speaker came
To take his place upon a low platform.

*To walk back into oneself
Step by step,
Towards the inner abode,
Is an unknown
Yet rewarding journey.*

        *Peace and fulfillment
Are the byproducts
Of this inner pilgrimage.*

7

The Beauty of Silence

What is the necessity of silence?
What is creative silence?
Can the mind be quiet?

What are we going to talk about this evening?

Come, why are you all suddenly silent?
Do you want me to talk so that you can listen?
What is your pleasure at this moment?

Let us explore this evening the process of talking,
And find out what silence is.
Perhaps we can look at the very act of talking,
To find out what it is that talks.
We know that there is the action of tongue and mouth,
Which produces the voice.
But do you know what stimulates the tongue
To generate speech?
What lies behind the tongue
That expresses itself through words?

Speech is a vibratory activity, but are you conscious
Of the movement of thought behind the tongue?
Are not the tongue and mouth vehicles of the psyche —
The mind, the thought process?
Can you see right now and watch how thought speaks,
How thought expresses itself in every word, every action?
Can you feel the movement of thought behind the word?

Is it necessary to talk all the time?
To be constantly active in thought?
Have you ever asked yourself
Why thought is chattering ceaselessly?
Are you aware of the compulsion of thought?

Do you think that you have a choice
In selecting your own thought and action?
Or does thought dictate its own course,
And use you as a mere vehicle for its expressions?

Do you have any control at all
Over this constant movement of thought-mind?

Don't you have the right to remain free from all thoughts?
And also the right to enjoy the freedom from them?
Can you look into yourself, ponder awhile,
And discover the truth of this matter?

Do you know the state, the unique existence
When the chattering of thought is totally absent?

What you call silence
Is only a period of non-verbalization.
That is the time when tongue and voice are quiet,

Simply the absence of speech.
But is that silence?

The state of silence is the absence of thought,
Not merely the absence of voice.
One can be mute and not necessarily be silent.
Willful and forceful subjugation is not silence.
Will can induce the state of non-thought for a moment,
But such a compulsion is not silence.

Silence happens
When the flight of thought is observed,
With sensitive polyangular attention,
Within one's own energy field.

Silence happens
When the flight of thought is observed,
And its trajectory followed, quietly and aloofly,
Without any attempt to arrest its thrust.

Silence happens
When the flight of thought is observed and understood
To be a mere mechanical reaction
Of old habit patterns,
And allowed to come to its natural ending.

Do you know the state of silence and its content?
Do you ever experience moments when there is no thought?
Do you know what the state of non-thought is?
Silence is primarily the negation of thought activity.
In silence the whole energy remains unruffled,
Quiet and serene within its own bounds;
Not chattering and scattering the energy,

Not throwing itself out through ego projections.
Such silence is the harmony of total energy within.

Are you ever completely silent?
Do you know this deeper inner silence
Of tranquil and harmonious energy?
Caught in the constant activity of what you call living,
You are always agitated, excited,
Concerned, hopeful or fearful.
Is that the only way of living?
Must the life energy be ceaselessly active,
Caught in riddles of thought-emotions,
Constantly disturbed by cerebral waves?

Is it not one of the functions of consciousness
To be also quiet, tranquil and serene?

Quietude, peace and tranquility are just words to you,
Are they not?
Have you ever experienced what tranquility is?
You are caught in constant, agitated waves of thoughts.
All of your life you spend your energy this way.
From childhood you have trained yourselves
To use your energy only in thought activity.
You have trained this mechanism of mind accordingly.
You have accepted this way, and never questioned it.

You never know the beauty of silence,
Which is so very comforting, aesthetic and mystical.
Silence is a state of fullness and contentment.
Silence permeates the perfume of the present.
Silence generates the joy of creative existence.

As you are now, sitting in this room,
Can you listen to silence, within yourself?
There is an art of listening to the inner quietude
And to the silence around you.
This whole place is so quiet.
Listen to the quiet, inside and outside.
Throw open all your senses, body and mind to listen.
Listen sensitively, intently and deeply.
With the totality of your being,
Experience the beauty of peace and tranquility,
Outside yourself, as well as within.
In such quietude thought has no place.
Feel it — you will experience how energetic
And refreshing the quality of silence is.

Why is thought active all the time?
By its very nature it is simply mechanical,
A compulsive, habitual momentum.
There are occasions when thought is necessary of course.
But is its function to be active constantly,
And never remain quiet?
Watch yourself, when you have free moments,
When there is no compelling need for action.
Surprisingly, you cannot remain quiet, even for sometime.
You pick up anything to occupy yourself.
Inadvertently you pick up any book or newspaper
Or infectiously switch on the T.V.
But the mind abhors to stay silent in thought and action.

Have you noticed how some people talk constantly
About themselves, about past happenings?
They pick up any small event of the past
And keep on talking about it excitedly,

Dramatizing every little aspect
Of people, things and situations.
Be aware of such a mind.

Such a talkative mind is essentially old.
Chattering is the first symptom
Of crystallization of the mind.
Such a person is truly old,
And lives mostly in memory-mind, in the past.
Peace is denied to such a person.
Chewing the memory is the easiest thing to do at any time.
It is the old and lethargic mind
That keeps itself occupied with bygone events.
Such a mind will never know what peace is,
What the flow of the mysterious present is,
What the tranquil order of energy is.

Do you know any other way of living
That is not based solely on thought-mind —
But is a movement of spontaneity:
The flow of eternity.

This energy flow, which is hidden within,
Is very subtle, sensitive and dynamic.
It is to be experienced
By the totality of one's own life force.
This energy flow is untouchable by thought.
It is nonverbal, silent and immaculate,
Uninterested in any plan of the mind.
But because of this constant movement of thought
The flow of silent energy within is denied.
Thought is the slayer of silence.

You take so much pride in the cultivation of thought
And in the constant use of it.
The more civilized you are,
The more intellectual you seem to become,
And the more indulgent you tend to be
In ideas and various fabrications of thought.
You never experience the elemental energy,
That which is devoid of thought.
Nor do you know the state of silence
Where creativity is born.

Silence of total energy is an experience of ecstasy.
It is not inaction, inertia or lethargy.
When the life force is free from the domination of thought,
It becomes very sensitive and potent,
Effervescent and dynamically active within.
Silence is not the right word to describe the state,
As it is so vibrant and spontaneous by its nature.
Silence is a fountain of new-dimensional force.
In silence resides the creative source.

Silence is the outcome of undivided energy,
Gathered and consolidated life force,
The foundation of wholeness,
The source of divinity and holiness.

Thought divides and limits the energy of life,
Channelling it into separate and exclusive drives.
Thought is a reaction from unfulfilled desire
Which moves in only one direction,
Driving towards its own fulfillment,
Excluding all other thoughts.
Each thought is a fragment,
A chip off the old log of life.

We are composed of hundreds and thousands of thoughts,
Each separate, interacting and contradicting the others.
With freedom from thought comes integration
Of the life energy, the invincible, unfragmented totality.
Then only one knows what peace is,
What the aesthetic beauty of silence is.

Can we bring about the integration of energy
To know its total action?
Energy itself is capable of acting on its own.

From profound silence emerges spiritual action,
A mystical, spontaneous expression,
Unlike the mechanical and compulsive drive of thought.
We do not know that kind of spiritual action
Because we are always engaged and divided
In emotional and logical interaction.
Isn't this the way we function?

Thought has its own utility,
But we live by the thought process alone
And never see its limitations.
We never aspire to go beyond the realm of thought.
We are missing the totality of life,
The creative spontaneity of it.

The action that springs from tranquil energy,
From silence, is total and complete.
It is an action of intuitive intelligence,
Which is impersonal, and thus is spiritual.
So there is a way to true action,
Without the dictation and drive of thought.
Right action takes place instantaneously,
Without the prompting of memory-mind.

Now thought throws you out into action
And you have no freedom at all.
You are just a captive of memory
With all its crude and subtle compulsions.

And what is after all this tiny
Yet so powerful thing called thought?
Have you ever wondered?
How does a thought arise? From where, and why?
Have you ever questioned,
Or explored, to find all about it?

Thought comes from somewhere
And makes you act, that is all.
You may reject one thought and accept another,
But you always work with some single thought.
And each time you are thrown into action
Only to fulfill that thought.
Yet you never question
The origin and validity of thought.
Inside yourself you are divided,
Harboring several contradictory thoughts.
Unknown and unwanted, ideas and images confront each other,
In a puzzle and jumble of interaction.

What is the foundation of thought?
Is thought not the residue of the past?
From unsatisfied experiences you have created a memory.
This memory is kept alive, pushing you, motivating you,
In the desperate effort toward its fulfillment.
Here lies the birth of a desire.

Then you naturally need the future — the time —
To fulfill the incomplete longing.

So thought creates a future, a hope, away from the past,
And thus you are in the cycle of time.

This cycle of memory-desire-fulfillment goes on and on,
Uninterrupted, with its own fast momentum,
Never giving you a moment, a gap or an interval.
Only the gap between two thoughts is the opening,
To enter the region of silence.

Silence is the gate to go beyond.

We are missing the aesthetic beauty of silence,
The fragrance of quietude and inner peace,
Because the mind has become overgrown and overactive.
It has captured us and the whole energy of life,
Going on and on ceaselessly,
Continuing with its mechanical momentum in time.

Your education and culture demand
That you be engaged by the mind constantly.
In the present culture of competitive commercial society,
There seems to be no room for silence.
We just continue in time, through hope,
Hopping and running around with pursuits of thought,
And that is what we call our civilized living.
But what is life without peace and freedom?
We are compelled, bound by thought, by desire, by emotion.
Now we need to discover a new way, a way of freedom,
A way of creativity, which brings wisdom,
Happiness and peace in living.
Then we will experience a unique energy,
And the state of freedom, of liberation,
Which is the highest state of living.

Then there will be no craving by thought
And no struggle to reach anywhere.
You will be fully in the silence of the moment,
Entrenched in profound peace of the present.
In silence alone can one capture the eternal moment.
This moment is the beginning and end of time,
The trickle of eternity.

Watch your talkative mind.
You will see the futility of its constant activity —
Thinking, talking, ceaselessly through thought.
Then you will wonder over thought.
You will realize the limitation and ignorance of thought.
You will no longer be enamoured by thought.
You will not like to be carried away by thought.
You will realize the necessity of non-thought.

Quietude and silence are not the negation of life,
But the regeneration of it.
Silence is the means
To elevate life energy to a timeless dimension.

Only in the present is the energy quiet and balanced,
Uncontaminated and vibrantly alive,
Sensitive enough to receive the unknown.

We have got to find this unknown dimension of life.
We need it very much right now.
The whole world is in desperate need
Of a new-dimensional consciousness,
So that human beings can live intelligently,
Creatively, spontaneously and lovingly,
And not just follow the ego pursuits mechanically.

When one begins to realize the limitation
Of all thought activity and ego drives,
The attachment and excitement drops.
The sensational pursuits stop.
One is left with a deep, profound silence.

Silence becomes eloquent and active.
Silence becomes intelligent and positive.
Action that springs from the depth of silence
Is spontaneous, truthful and universal.
It is immaculate, timeless and spiritual.

Silence is the means and silence is the end.
Creative silence is the ultimate challenge.

Silence is the sap that rejuvenates life.
Silence is the source of eternal life.

The Experience of Eternal

A meeting place was selected under a huge oak tree,
Near a high cliff overlooking the Pacific Ocean.
It was shady and cool even on this summer day.
The cliff was surrounded by water on three sides,
And the vast ocean lay beyond in endless distance.
The deep blue sky filled the wide horizon,
Giving a sense of enormity and the touch of eternity.

The expanse of sky everywhere,
And no point for the eye to rest anywhere,
Created a feeling of timelessness.
One looked over the cliff, the end of land,
To face the horizon and the unknown beyond.

The technicians were ready with their video cameras,
Light reflectors, and sound equipment.
They were whispering amongst themselves
About the lighting conditions and exposure.
People arrived for the meeting in colorful clothing.
All was set for the talk
And the shooting began in pin drop silence.

You are the changeless
You are the deathless
You are the eternal
Ancient one.

Let that eternal within you
Be yours.
Let that immaculate experience
Of timelessness within you
Be yours.

8

The Experience of Eternal

Can we experience the totality of life?
How do we discover the eternal present?
Are you not divine by nature?

Friends, greetings on this fine morning.
It is a very beautiful day.
Nature looks so fresh and new.
Perhaps nature is always new.
Only we have to have eyes, ears
And all the senses open
To look newly and freshly at it.

Isn't it that peace and harmony
Are the very basis of beauty in nature?
See, the whole nature is so tranquil,
Contented, creative and alive.
It is so joyful, serene and harmonious.
The sun, water and air blend together
So well to create a symphony in nature.
Such a blending is creative existence.

Co-operation and mingling together
Of all the elements of nature
Create the outer harmony which is perfection.
Here lies the secret of beauty
And creative newness of nature.

Perhaps the same is true with a person.
Harmonious blending
Of all the elements and forces in man
Generates the joy and happiness in living.
Harmony of the total energy of man
Brings about this wholeness,
And a sense of ecstasy which is happiness.
Wisdom is the outcome of such whole energy.
Intuitive intelligence,
Which is impersonal understanding of life,
Is the expression of total energy.
Such an undivided, unfragmented energy flow within
Is the seat and source of wisdom.

The source of wisdom is hidden within.
But the ceaseless activity of the mind,
The constant chattering of thought,
Is the hindrance and burden.

The thought process is a divisive mechanism.
Every thought is a fragmentary
And exclusive drive of the ego.
So we cannot rely on the mind
To bring about the wholeness in life energy.

Do you know what the totality of life is?
The unfragmented, invincible individuality?

Totality is a harmonious blending of a whole man,
Undivided by any environmental,
Cultural or psychological conditionings.
Such an uninfluenced person
Is open, sensitive and receptive
To meet life as it is.

Do you ever listen to the song of the birds?
Are you attentive to the shine on the leaf,
The reflected light of the sun?
Can you see the gentle breeze
Playing on the calm surface of the lake?
And the wind dancing with the blade of grass?
Can you feel the wind carrying a mild fragrance
From freshly blooming flowers?
Are you sensitive enough to see the play
Of light and shade on the green meadows?

Look at that tall tree in the foreground,
Giving the sense of depth
To create a three-dimensional effect
For a picturesque green landscape.
Are you awake to see the different designs,
Forms and colors in nature?
Are you conscious of geometric patterns
And artistry in plants, leaves and flowers?

Who creates such a beautiful nature?
Is there anyone to create it?
Perhaps there is no one to create
Apart from the creation.
Creator and creation are one.
Beauty and experience are one.

The sense of separation, as subject and object,
And the feeling of time and distance,
Are the result of a limitation of the senses,
Which is the cause of ignorance.

Have you watched any time
A bird sitting on the top of a tree
And singing by itself?
Have you noticed quietly,
How happily he sings alone?
His song is an expression of joy.
And why is the bird so joyful?
Is he happy because he received some fortune?
Does he sing merrily
Because he expects something?
Certainly not!
The bird is just with himself.

To be happy is to be in communion
With one's own total being.
The bird lives in his creative moment,
Fully enjoying the richness of the present.

To be in the moment of the present fully
Is to be happy.
There, one's very existence is the state
Of peace and joy.

The creative present is the source
And substance of freedom and happiness.
In the discovery of such fullness of the moment
Lies the great secret of life.

This experience of the moment
Is creative and dynamic, and yet very quiet.
Such quietude is the absence of ego-mind.
Freedom from all ego functionings
Is the state of meditation,
In which one remains very humble and simple.

Simplicity and humility are the means
To invite divinity.
Be simple to watch
And humble to accept whatever you are.
Accepting life with alert watchfulness,
In every fresh moment of the present,
Is the way of meditation.

Meditation is the state of total being.
In this totality of being
One experiences profound peace
And unbounded intelligence.
In this state of intelligence
One is free from all strivings,
Conflicts and fears generated by the mind.

Thought-free energy remains tranquil,
Sensitive and dynamically alert
To catch the whisper that flashes
From beyond the frontiers of mind.
Such a state of tranquil attention,
In the present, is meditation.

Meditation is a state of attentive observation
Of all promptings of intellect and emotions,
While remaining awake and free within.

The Experience of Eternal

Meditation is not
The concentration of thought anywhere,
But the full attention of sensitivity everywhere.
A constant vigilance in the present
Concerning all of the mind movements
Is meditation.

An experience of wholeness of being
Is meditation.
Meditation is the means
To step beyond the confines of the mind,
Towards peace and freedom from time.

But are you ever peaceful and tranquil within?
To feel the ecstasy and freedom of living?
Why is it that you are incapable of this freedom?
Why is this thought-mind so dominant,
To keep you in bondage,
Encaged in a psychological prison?
Why do you basically put up with this situation?
Is there any way of getting free
From ego domination?

On this planet earth,
The human being is the only creature
Who is constantly intoxicated
By his ego actions,
Struggling ceaselessly for perfection
Through his own petty little dreams,
Remaining ignorant of life's eternal stream.

Is it possible to come upon
The creative state of freedom,
Like the bird who sings for no reason?

The beauty of his song is that
It is sung for no one,
With no intention of recognition from anyone,
And utterly unmindful of passers-by.
For the bird, song is the way,
Its life and fulfillment.

Such a creative life of happiness
Is freely available to all of us,
At all times and everywhere.
But where are we?
Are we on the right path?
Are we aware of that inner aesthetic stream?
Are we working towards it?
He who aspires and works for it
With the full potential of his life energy
Shall certainly have it.

The source of happiness and peace
Is the abode — the center of life.
It is so near, right in yourself,
Within your spiritual heart.
Take a look, turn within, with all of your energy.

Your abode may seem very far,
And yet, it is so near.
He who will earnestly move within,
With all his life force, shall reach.
Like a flock of homesick birds,
Flying eagerly back to their mountain nest,
Let the body, mind and all your senses
Flock together for the journey back,
Towards your eternal home.

Can you look into yourself
At all the wandering thoughts,
Without getting caught in their expression?
Can you aloofly observe
The complex interaction of thought-emotion?

Let thoughts be wandering, as they do,
    But remain watchful and quiet in you.
Let outer be moving and agitating, too,
    But inner be calm and quiet.
Let thought-mind remain busy and scattered,
    But consciousness remain quiet.
Like the solar system whirling around,
    Yet the sun at the center is quiet.

Let senses pursue their cravings,
    But energy remain quiet.
Let mind do its wandering,
    But the observation be quiet.
Like waves breaking on the surface,
    Yet the ocean below is quiet.
The clouds do wander everywhere,
    But the sky remains serene and quiet.

Let the circumference of your life be active,
    But the center remain vigilant and quiet.
Let the chattering of mind go on and on,
    Only keep perception aloof and calm.
The more intensely you begin to watch,
    The more quiet and humble you begin to become.

You are the vastness of the sky,
    And not fragmented wandering clouds.

You are the sensitive, attentive witness,
    Not transient memories nor thoughts.
You are the deep and profound ocean,
    Not shallow and tiny waves.
You are the supreme steadfast sun,
    Not circling satellite thoughts.
You — You are the stable, eternal inner,
    Not the fluctuating, perishable outer.

You are the vastness, you are the changeless,
You are the eternal ancient one.
    You are that!
Let that eternal within you be yours.
Let that immutable experience of timelessness
    Within you, be yours.

    Awake, arise!
This hour is precious, this moment is yours.
Ponder, meditate and realize
Your eternal, divine nature.